THRIVING ALONE

A guide to solo parenting after Separation and Divorce

Lynn Crawford

Thriving Alone: A guide to solo parenting after
Separation and Divorce

ISBN 978-1-915962-42-3
First published by Compass-Publishing UK 2024

Printed in the United Kingdom

A catalogue version of the book can be found at the British Library

Interior layout by The Book Refinery Ltd
www.TheBookRefinery.com

Cover designed by ©
Cover photo © i-stock

This publication is designed to provide authoritative information for single parents. It is sold under the express understanding that any decisions or actions you take as a result of reading this book must be based on your judgement and will be at your sole risk. The author will not be held responsible for the consequences of any actions and/or decisions taken as a result of any information given or recommendations made.

I would like to dedicate this book to my wonderful three children Aidan, Brooke and Elena who are my reason to get up everyday and have kept me going even through the darkest of times.

I would also like to give a huge thank you to my mum who is my rock and is so supportive to me and my children.

CONTENTS

1 - INTRODUCTION 9
How to read this book 11

2 - UNDERSTANDING SOLO PARENTING AFTER DIVORCE 13
The Challenges of Solo Parenting 13
The Emotional Journey of Divorce 15
Navigating Co-Parenting Agreements 17

3 - BUILDING A SUPPORT NETWORK 20
The Importance of Emotional Support 20
Seeking Professional Help 22
Connecting with Other Solo Parents 24

4 - PRIORITISING SELF-CARE 26
Making Time for Yourself 26
Managing Stress and Anxiety 28
Establishing Healthy Boundaries 30

5 - DEVELOPING A CO-PARENTING RELATIONSHIP 32
Effective Communication Strategies 32
Creating a Co-Parenting Plan 34
Dealing with Conflict and Disagreements 36

6 - THRIVING FINANCIALLY AS A SOLO PARENT 39
Budgeting and Financial Planning 39
Seeking Child Support and Spousal Maintenance 40

7 - NURTURING YOUR CHILDREN'S WELL-BEING 45
Supporting Their Emotional Needs 45
Co-Parenting Discipline Strategies 47
Facilitating Healthy Relationships with the Other Parent 49

8 - CREATING A HAPPY AND STABLE HOME ENVIRONMENT 52
Establishing Routines and Structures 52
Managing Household Responsibilities 54
Promoting a Positive and Supportive Atmosphere 56

9 - BALANCING WORK AND PARENTING 58
Exploring Flexible Work Options 58
Managing Time and Priorities 60
Seeking Childcare Solutions 62

10 - MOVING FORWARD AND EMBRACING SINGLE PARENTHOOD 64
Embracing Your New Identity 64
Setting Goals and Creating a Vision for the Future 66
Finding Joy and Happiness in Solo Parenting 67

11 - CO-PARENTING CHALLENGES AND SOLUTIONS 70
Dealing with Difficult Ex-Partners 70
Handling Parental Alienation 72
Resolving Co-Parenting Conflicts in a Healthy Way 74

12 - HELPING YOUR CHILDREN ADJUST AND THRIVE 77
Supporting Their Emotional Healing 77
Providing Stability and Consistency 79
Encouraging Their Growth and Independence 81

13 - OVERCOMING LONELINESS AND FINDING CONNECTION 83
Combating Feelings of Isolation 83
Engaging in Community Activities and Organisations 85
Seeking Support from Solo Parenting Groups 87

14 - RECLAIMING YOUR LIFE AND PURSUING PERSONAL GOALS 89
Rediscovering Your Passions and Hobbies 89
Building a Supportive Social Network 91
Setting and Achieving Personal Milestones 93

15 - NAVIGATING DATING AND ROMANTIC RELATIONSHIPS 95
Exploring New Relationships 95
Introducing a New Partner to Your Children 97
Balancing Love and Parenting Responsibilities 99

16 - CELEBRATING YOUR STRENGTHS AND ACCOMPLISHMENTS 101
Reflecting on Your Journey 101
Acknowledging Your Growth as a Solo Parent 103
Embracing a Positive Future 105

CONCLUSION 108

WHERE NEXT? 110

ABOUT THE AUTHOR 111

INTRODUCTION

Welcome to *Thriving Alone: A Guide to Solo Parenting After Separation and Divorce.*

After being an army wife for 22 years I suddenly found myself a solo parent of 3 children aged 3, 9 and 11. It was one of the hardest challenges I ever had to face. Being strong for your children whilst your heart is breaking is a difficult situation to deal with. Not only did we lose the family unit we'd known, we also had to vacate our army residence with 90 days notice which meant that the children and I also lost our home, our support bubble, our community, and friends who had become family over the years.

Separation, whether from a partner or spouse, often plunges us into a whirlwind of emotional turbulence and uncertainty. One of the primary reasons we struggle with separation is the profound sense of loss it entails. Beyond the dissolution of a relationship, separation disrupts the familiar rhythms of life, shattering dreams and expectations for the future. Moreover, the intricate web of emotions—grief, anger, guilt, and fear—can overwhelm even the most resilient souls, leaving you grappling with a profound sense of disorientation. Additionally, separation often brings about practical challenges, from financial strain to logistical complexities, further exacerbating the emotional strain. ultimately, the journey through separation is fraught with hurdles, yet it also presents opportunities for growth, resilience, and ultimately, the rediscovery of one's inner strength.

Navigating the complexities of solo parenting can be a daunting journey, filled with uncertainties and challenges. Whether you're facing the aftermath of a separation or divorce, this book is here to provide you with the support, guidance, and empowerment you need to not just survive, but to thrive as a solo parent. I wish this had been available to me when going through it myself. Drawing from my personal experience and insights, this book offers practical strategies, emotional support, and valuable resources to help you navigate the ups and downs of single parenthood with confidence and grace.

As you embark on this transformative journey, remember that you are not alone. Countless individuals including myself have walked this path before you, and our wisdom, resilience, and triumphs serve as beacons of hope and inspiration. Together, we will explore the challenges that you may encounter as a solo parent, from co-parenting dynamics to financial management, and beyond. More importantly, we will uncover the hidden opportunities for growth, healing, and fulfillment that lie within this unique chapter of your life. So, take a deep breath, trust in your inner strength, and let's embark on this journey together, towards a future where you not only survive, but thrive as a solo parent.

Within the pages of this book you'll find invaluable insights and practical strategies to navigate the intricate journey of solo parenting and co-parenting with grace and resilience. This book offers a roadmap for fostering effective communication, managing conflicts constructively, and establishing healthy boundaries with a former partner, all while prioritising the well-being of the children involved. By providing you with tools to navigate the challenges of co-parenting, this guide empowers you to create a nurturing and stable environment for your children to thrive. Through fostering cooperation, consistency, and mutual respect, readers can ensure that your children emerge from the separation process with a sense of security, emotional resilience, and the knowledge that they are loved and supported, no matter the circumstances.

HOW TO READ THIS BOOK

Depending on where you are with your separation or divorce journey, there may be chapters that stand out and you are drawn to those first.

I've written this book so that you can dip in and out, so feel free to skip straight to that part.

There may also be chapters that you haven't thought of, or are struggling with. It might be easy to avoid dealing with these subjects, but I urge you to read, absorb and take small steps to resolve any conflict or hard to deal with issues. Feel free to lend the book to your ex partner if you think it'll help!

You can also find more information about how to join my community at the back of the book.

Chapter 1

UNDERSTANDING SOLO PARENTING AFTER DIVORCE

THE CHALLENGES OF SOLO PARENTING

Solo parenting after a divorce can be an overwhelming and daunting task. As a solo parent, you face unique challenges that can test your strength and resilience. Understanding these challenges and finding effective ways to navigate through them is crucial to ensure a healthy and thriving environment for both you and your children. In this section, we will explore the various challenges of solo parenting after divorce and provide you with practical guidance to overcome them.

One of the most significant challenges of solo parenting is the overwhelming responsibility that falls solely on your shoulders. From making important decisions to managing household chores and finances, the weight of these responsibilities can feel suffocating at times. It's essential to develop effective time management and organisational skills to maintain a balanced and fulfilling life.

Another challenge is coping with the emotional impact of the divorce while simultaneously providing emotional support to your children. Dealing with your own feelings of grief, anger, or loneliness can be challenging, but it's equally important to create a safe and nurturing environment where your children can express their emotions. Seeking therapy or joining support groups can be immensely beneficial in processing your own emotions and learning healthy ways to support your children through this difficult time.

Financial struggles are yet another challenge faced by many solo parents. Going from a dual-income household to a single income can put a strain on your finances. Creating a realistic budget and seeking financial assistance, if necessary, can help alleviate some of the financial stress and ensure the well-being of your family.

Sometimes also having to move with the children from the family home which in itself is another huge life changing event.

Balancing work and parenting responsibilities can also be a significant challenge. Juggling a career and the demands of solo parenting requires careful planning and time management. Prioritising your children's needs while also pursuing your own professional goals is very important. Establishing a support network of friends, family, or fellow solo parents can provide much-needed assistance and understanding during challenging times.

Additionally, solo parents often struggle with feelings of guilt and self-doubt. It's important to remember that you're doing the best you can under challenging circumstances. Seeking self-care, practicing self-compassion, and celebrating your successes, no matter how small, can help combat these negative emotions.

Solo parenting comes with its own set of challenges. Identifying and acknowledging these challenges is the first step towards overcoming them. By developing effective coping strategies, seeking support, and practicing self-care, you can thrive as a solo parent and create a nurturing environment where both you and your children can grow and flourish.

> You're not alone in this journey – there is a vast community of solo parents who are facing similar challenges and ready to offer support and guidance along the way.

THE EMOTIONAL JOURNEY OF DIVORCE

Divorce is a deeply personal and emotional experience that can turn your world upside down. As a solo parent, navigating the emotional journey of divorce can be overwhelming and challenging. In this next section we will explore the various emotions you may encounter during this process and provide strategies to help you thrive.

One of the first emotions you may experience is grief. Divorce represents the loss of a relationship, dreams, and the life you once knew. It's essential to acknowledge and allow yourself to grieve this loss. Give yourself permission to feel the pain, sadness, and anger that may arise. Surround yourself with a support system of friends, family, or a therapist who can provide a safe space for you to express your emotions.

During the emotional journey of divorce, it's common to experience a roller coaster of emotions. One day, you may feel optimistic about the future, and the next, overwhelming despair. It's important to remember that these emotions are normal and part of the healing process. Be patient with yourself and practice self-compassion as you navigate through these ups and downs.

Additionally, it's imperative to focus on self-care during this emotional journey. Prioritise activities that bring you joy and help you heal. This could include practicing mindfulness, engaging in hobbies, exercise, or spending time with loved ones. Taking care of your emotional well-being will not only benefit you but also positively impact your ability to parent effectively.

As you move forward, it's vital to develop healthy coping mechanisms to manage stress and anxiety. Journaling, meditation, or seeking professional help can provide you with tools to navigate through challenging emotions. Seeking support is a sign of strength, and reaching out for help is an important step in your healing journey.

Finally, embrace the concept of personal growth. Divorce can be an opportunity for self-discovery and reinvention. Take this time to reflect on your values, goals, and aspirations. Rediscover your passions and set new intentions for your life. Find your identity again, sometimes it becomes lost in your journey as a wife and mother. By focusing on personal growth, you'll not only heal from the emotional impact of divorce but also create a fulfilling and thriving life as a solo parent.

Remember, the emotional journey of divorce is unique to each individual. Allow yourself the time and space to heal, and be patient with the process. By acknowledging your emotions, practicing self-care, seeking support, and embracing personal growth, you will navigate through this challenging phase and emerge as a stronger, more resilient solo parent.

NAVIGATING CO-PARENTING AGREEMENTS

When it comes to parenting, one of the most crucial aspects to consider is establishing a solid co-parenting agreement. Co-parenting can be challenging and emotionally draining, but with the right approach and dedication, it can also be a rewarding experience for both you and your children. Let me now explain the essential components of creating and navigating successful co-parenting agreements, which will provide valuable insights and practical tips for solo parents like yourself.

It's imperative to approach co-parenting with a positive and cooperative mindset. Despite any lingering resentment or animosity towards your ex-spouse, focusing on your children's best interests should be your top priority. Establishing clear communication channels and maintaining open lines of dialogue with your ex-partner will be vital in ensuring that your co-parenting journey is as smooth as possible.

Sometimes this isn't possible, especially if one of the parents has controlling, bullying or narcissistic tendencies. Not every divorce journey is the same.

In creating a co-parenting agreement, it's essential to define the roles and responsibilities of each parent. This includes establishing a schedule for visitation, holidays, and vacations, as well as determining how decisions regarding your children's education, healthcare, and extracurricular activities will be made. By setting clear guidelines and expectations, you can reduce misunderstandings and conflicts, providing stability and consistency for your children.

Flexibility is another key aspect of successful co-parenting. Recognise that circumstances may change, and being open to modifications in the agreement can help accommodate new situations that arise. Don't forget the ultimate goal is to create a nurturing and supportive environment for your children, and adapting to their evolving needs is a big part of that.

Additionally, we can try to foster a healthy co-parenting relationship with your ex-spouse, but only if you're able to do so. Avoid involving your children in adult conflicts, and instead, focus on promoting positive interactions between them and their other parent. Encourage regular communication and cooperation, as well as respecting each other's parenting choices and decisions.

Throughout your co-parenting journey prioritise your own self-care. Solo parenting can be overwhelming, and it's important to take care of yourself physically, mentally, and emotionally. Seek support from friends, family, or support groups, and consider professional help if needed. Taking care of yourself will not only benefit you but also enhance your ability to be an effective parent.

Navigating co-parenting agreements, if possible, will help you to thrive in raising your children.

If both parents can work with a positive mindset, establish clear guidelines, foster flexibility this can help to promote a healthy relationship with your ex-spouse. By prioritising self-care, you can create a nurturing and harmonious environment for your children. You shouldn't have to be alone on this journey, with the right strategies and support if you have them, you can thrive.

There will be times when it's not possible to Co parent and the parenting is left to one parent. When the resident parent doesn't have that free weekend or a break in the holidays it can be exhausting both emotionally and physically. Make sure you have a support network of friends or family that you can turn to for support.

Chapter 2

BUILDING A SUPPORT NETWORK

THE IMPORTANCE OF EMOTIONAL SUPPORT

In the tumultuous journey of solo parenting after divorce, emotional support plays a pivotal role in helping solo parents navigate the challenges and uncertainties they face. The importance of emotional support cannot be overstated, as it provides solace, strength, and resilience during these trying times. This chapter delves into the significance of emotional support for solo parents and offers guidance on seeking and nurturing such support networks.

Solo parents often find themselves overwhelmed with the demands of single-handedly raising their children. The emotional toll of divorce can be immense, leaving them feeling isolated and vulnerable. Emotional support acts as a lifeline, offering a safe space to express feelings, share experiences, and seek guidance from others who have walked a similar path.

One of the key benefits of emotional support is the validation it provides. Solo parents may find themselves questioning their decisions or feeling guilt-ridden about the divorce. By connecting with others who have experienced similar challenges, they gain reassurance that they are not alone and that their emotions are valid. This validation helps solo parents overcome self-doubt, boosting their self-esteem and empowering them to make sound choices for themselves and their children.

Emotional support also aids in building resilience. Through supportive relationships, solo parents gain the strength to persevere through adversity. Friends, family, or support groups can offer practical advice, coping strategies, and a listening ear during difficult moments. By sharing the burden of solo parenting, solo parents can alleviate stress and prevent burnout, allowing them to be more present and nurturing to their children.

Moreover, emotional support networks provide a sense of belonging and camaraderie. When solo parents engage with others who understand their unique challenges, they form connections that transcend their immediate circumstances. These connections offer opportunities for shared experiences, shared resources, and the formation of lifelong friendships. Additionally, support networks can provide access to professional help, such as therapists or counsellors, who specialise in assisting solo parents.

To cultivate emotional support, solo parents can also proactively seek out communities, both online and offline, that cater to solo parenting. Engaging in various activities, such as support groups, workshops, or online forums, enables solo parents to connect with others, exchange stories, and gather valuable insights. Being open and honest about their experiences can help solo parents build deep and meaningful relationships with individuals who truly understand their journey.

Emotional support is a critical ingredient in the recipe for successful solo parenting. It offers validation, resilience, and a sense of belonging, empowering solo parents to navigate the challenges with grace and determination. By actively seeking and nurturing emotional support networks, solo parents can create a solid foundation for their personal growth and create a nurturing environment for their children.

SEEKING PROFESSIONAL HELP

One of the most challenging aspects is navigating the emotional and psychological toll it can take on you and your children. It's perfectly normal to feel overwhelmed, stressed, or even lost during this transition. However, there is no shame in seeking professional help to guide you through this difficult time. In fact, reaching out to a therapist or counsellor can be one of the most proactive steps you can take towards healing and rebuilding a fulfilling life for yourself and your children.

Therapy can provide a safe and unbiased space for you to express your emotions, discuss your concerns, and explore effective coping strategies. A skilled therapist specialising in solo parenting after divorce can guide you through the complexities of co-parenting, help you navigate your own emotions, and provide valuable insights into how to create a stable and loving home environment for your children.

Additionally, therapy can be immensely beneficial for your children. Divorce can have a profound impact on their emotional well-being, and having a professional to talk to can help them process their feelings and adjust to the new family dynamic. Through play therapy, art therapy, or simply having someone to listen to them, children can gain a deeper understanding of their emotions and develop healthier ways to express themselves.

In addition to therapy, seeking professional help may also include consulting with a financial advisor or solicitor who specialises in Family Law and can give you advice on divorce and custody matters. These professionals can offer valuable guidance on managing your finances, understanding your rights and responsibilities, and ensuring that you're making informed decisions for the future.

Getting professional help shows a commitment to the well-being of yourself and your children. It takes courage to acknowledge that you may need support and guidance during this challenging time. By reaching out to professionals who specialise in solo parenting after divorce, you're taking active steps towards not just surviving, but thriving as a solo parent.

Seeking professional help can be instrumental in your journey. It can provide you with the necessary tools, support, and guidance to navigate the emotional, psychological, and practical challenges that arise during this transition. Remember, you don't have to face this journey alone – there are professionals out there who are dedicated to helping you and your children thrive.

CONNECTING WITH OTHER SOLO PARENTS

One of the most challenging aspects of solo parenting after a divorce is the feeling of isolation. It can be difficult to navigate this new chapter in your life without the support and understanding of others who are going through a similar experience. That's why connecting with other solo parents is so beneficial to your well-being and success as a single parent.

The first step in connecting with other solo parents is to seek out support groups or organisations that cater specifically to this niche. These groups provide a safe and non-judgmental space where you can freely express your thoughts, concerns, and challenges. Sharing your experiences with others who understand firsthand what you're going through can be therapeutic and empowering.

Online forums and social media groups are also a great way to connect with other solo parents. These platforms allow you to interact with individuals from all over the world who have faced similar struggles and triumphs. You can exchange advice, share resources, and offer support to one another. The beauty of online communities is that they are accessible 24/7, so you can find support whenever you need it.

Additionally, consider reaching out to your local community. Look for parenting groups, community centres, or organisations that offer programs specifically designed for single parents. Participating in these activities can help you meet other solo parents who live in your area, providing opportunities for face-to-face connections and friendships.

When connecting with other solo parents, keep in mind that not everyone will have the same experiences or perspectives.

It's important to be open-minded and respectful of different parenting styles and life choices. Embrace the diversity within the solo parenting community, as it can broaden your understanding and help you gain new insights.

> Remember, connecting with other solo parents isn't just about receiving support; it's also about giving support. By sharing your own experiences and offering guidance to others, you can make a positive impact in someone else's life. Through these connections, you will realise that you're not alone in your journey and that there is strength in unity.

In conclusion, connecting with other solo parents is essential as a single parent. Seek out support groups, online communities, and local resources to find like-minded individuals who can offer guidance, understanding, and friendship. By connecting with others and being part of a community, you will find the support and encouragement you need to navigate the challenges of the next chapter of your parenting journey.

Chapter 3

PRIORITISING SELF-CARE

MAKING TIME FOR YOURSELF

One of the most essential aspects of solo parenting is learning to prioritise self-care and making time for yourself. As a solo parent, it's easy to get caught up in the demands of raising children single-handedly, managing work, and handling household responsibilities. However, neglecting your own needs can lead to burnout and hinder your ability to provide the best care for your children. Let's explore how to carve out time for yourself amidst the chaos of this next stage of your life.

Firstly, recognise that taking care of yourself isn't selfish but rather a necessity. By making time for self-care, you're ensuring your own well-being, which in turn benefits your children. Begin by setting boundaries and communicating your needs to your children. Explain to them that you also require time alone to recharge and rejuvenate. This will help them understand the importance of respecting your personal space.

Next, create a weekly schedule that includes dedicated "me-time." Block out specific hours or days in which you engage in activities that bring you joy and relaxation. Whether it's reading a book, practicing yoga, going for a walk in nature, or pursuing a hobby, make sure to prioritise activities that recharge your energy and bring a sense of fulfillment.

Additionally, consider reaching out to your support network. Seek assistance from family members, friends, or even professional services like babysitters or parenting co-ops. By having reliable help, you can allocate more time for yourself without feeling guilty or overwhelmed. Remember, it takes a village to raise a child, and there is no shame in seeking support.

Moreover, take advantage of technology to streamline your responsibilities. Utilise online grocery delivery services, meal planning apps, or consider hiring a cleaning service to free up time for yourself. By outsourcing some tasks, you can create more space in your daily routine to focus on self-care.

Lastly, embrace the power of saying "no." Solo parenting often means juggling numerous responsibilities, and it's easy to take on more than you can handle. Learn to decline unnecessary commitments and prioritise your personal well-being. Saying no allows you to protect your time and energy, ensuring you have enough to give to both yourself and your children.

Making time for yourself is vital for solo parents navigating the challenging journey of parenting. By prioritising self-care, setting boundaries, seeking support, and embracing the art of saying no, solo parents can find balance, recharge their energy, and provide the best care for their children. Remember, investing in yourself is an investment in your children's future.

MANAGING STRESS AND ANXIETY

As a solo parent, navigating the challenges of single-handedly raising children after a divorce can be overwhelming. The added responsibilities, financial strain, and emotional upheaval can often lead to increased stress and anxiety. However, you must prioritise your well-being and develop effective strategies to manage these feelings. Let's now explore various techniques to help you cope with stress and anxiety, allowing you to thrive in your solo parenting journey.

Firstly, it's important to acknowledge and accept your emotions. Divorce is a significant life event that can trigger a rollercoaster of feelings. Take time to process your emotions and understand that it's normal to experience stress and anxiety during this transition. Recognising and accepting your emotions is the first step towards managing them effectively.

Next, establishing a support network is essential. Surround yourself with understanding friends, family members, or support groups specifically designed for single parents. Sharing your experiences, worries, and achievements with others who have gone through similar situations can offer immense comfort and reassurance. Additionally, consider seeking professional help such as therapy or counselling. A therapist can provide you with valuable coping strategies and a safe space to express your emotions.

Practicing self-care is paramount when managing stress and anxiety. Set aside time each day for activities that bring you joy and relaxation. Engage in exercise, meditation, or hobbies that allow you to unwind and recharge. Prioritising your physical and mental well-being will not only benefit you but also positively impact your ability to parent effectively.

Incorporating stress management techniques into your daily routine can also alleviate anxiety. Deep breathing exercises, mindfulness, and visualisation techniques can help reduce stress levels and promote a sense of calm. Consider exploring different relaxation techniques until you find what works best for you.

Lastly, maintain a healthy work-life balance. It can be tempting to overcompensate for the absence of the other parent by taking on extra responsibilities. Set boundaries and ensure you have time for yourself and your children. Allocating specific times for work, household chores, and quality time with your children can help reduce stress and prevent burnout.

Remember, managing stress and anxiety is an ongoing process. Be patient with yourself and allow room for self-compassion. By implementing these strategies, you can cultivate resilience, find joy in your solo parenting journey, and create a nurturing environment for your children as you thrive alone.

ESTABLISHING HEALTHY BOUNDARIES

One of the most important aspects of solo parenting is establishing healthy boundaries. As a solo parent, you may find yourself juggling numerous responsibilities and emotions, which can be overwhelming at times. However, by setting clear boundaries, you can create a stable and nurturing environment for both yourself and your children.

Boundaries are the invisible lines that define where you end and others begin. They act as a protective shield, ensuring that you and your children have the space and emotional well-being required to thrive. Establishing healthy boundaries involves setting limits, communicating your needs, and respecting yourself and others.

Firstly, it's essential to set boundaries with your ex-partner. This may involve establishing rules for communication, scheduling visitation, or discussing financial responsibilities. By clearly defining these boundaries, you can minimise conflict and create a more harmonious co-parenting relationship.

Setting boundaries with your children is equally important. While it's natural to want to protect and provide for them, it's all about getting a balance between being there for them and allowing them to develop their independence. Establishing consistent routines, enforcing rules, and encouraging open communication will help foster a healthy parent-child dynamic.

Another aspect of boundary-setting is taking care of yourself. As a solo parent, it's easy to neglect your own needs while focusing on your children. However, prioritising self-care is vital for your well-being. This may involve setting aside time for hobbies, seeking support from friends or support groups, or practicing self-compassion. Remember, taking care of yourself isn't selfish – it's necessary for you to be the best parent you can be.

Lastly, it's imperative to set boundaries with others in your life. Well-meaning family members and friends may offer advice or try to intervene in your parenting decisions. While their intentions may be good, it's essential to assert your autonomy and make decisions that align with your values and beliefs. Communicate your boundaries respectfully and assertively, ensuring that your own judgment is respected.

To summarise this chapter, establishing healthy boundaries is a fundamental aspect of solo parenting. By setting clear limits with your ex-partner, children, and others in your life, you can create a stable and nurturing environment for yourself and your children. Remember, boundaries act as a protective shield, ensuring your emotional well-being and allowing you to thrive as a solo parent.

Chapter 4

DEVELOPING A CO-PARENTING RELATIONSHIP

EFFECTIVE COMMUNICATION STRATEGIES

Effective communication is critical for single parents navigating the challenges of parenting after a divorce. As a solo parent, if it's possible try to establish clear and open lines of communication to ensure the well-being of your children and foster a positive co-parenting relationship with your ex-spouse. This chapter will explain various strategies that can help you communicate effectively in the context of single parenting.

One of the most important communication strategies for solo parents is to prioritise active listening. When engaging in conversations with your ex-spouse or your children, make a conscious effort to fully understand their perspective without interrupting or judging. Active listening involves providing verbal and non-verbal cues that you're attentively listening, such as nodding your head and maintaining eye contact. This approach can help create a safe space for open and honest communication.

Another effective strategy for communication is to use "I" statements instead of "you" statements. By expressing your thoughts and feelings using "I" statements, you avoid sounding accusatory or confrontational. For example, instead of saying, "You never spend enough time with the kids," you can say, "I feel concerned about the amount of time the kids spend with you." This shift in language can lead to more constructive conversations and reduce conflicts.

Utilising technology can also enhance communication between solo parents and their ex-spouses. Platforms such as co-parenting apps or shared calendars can help coordinate schedules, share important information, and maintain ongoing communication without direct face-to-face interaction. These tools can provide a structured and organised approach to co-parenting, ensuring that both parents are informed and involved.

In addition, setting boundaries and establishing clear expectations is essential for effective communication. Solo parents should communicate their needs and boundaries to their ex-spouse and children in a respectful and assertive manner. By doing so, you can create a cooperative and mutually respectful environment that benefits everyone involved.

Lastly, seeking professional help through family counselling or mediation can be invaluable for improving communication between co-parents. A neutral third party can facilitate discussions, provide guidance, and help resolve conflicts in a constructive manner. Professional intervention can also help solo parents develop effective communication skills that promote healthy co-parenting relationships.

Therefore, effective communication is vital for navigating the challenges of parenting. By prioritising active listening, using "I" statements, utilising technology, setting boundaries, and seeking professional help, solo parents can enhance their communication strategies and foster healthier co-parenting relationships. Strong communication skills not only benefit the children but also contribute to the overall well-being of the solo parent.

CREATING A CO-PARENTING PLAN

One of the most pivotal aspects of solo parenting is establishing a strong and effective co-parenting plan. This plan will serve as a roadmap for navigating the complexities of raising children in separate households, ensuring their well-being and maintaining a positive co-parenting relationship. Let's now look at the essential steps to create a co-parenting plan that works for both parents and, most importantly, the children.

It's understandable that this chapter may not apply to many of you solo parents as there are some situations where one parent does not see the children and does not wish to be involved in their day to day upbringing. For those of you who are co-parenting or trying to co-parent this chapter will be valuable for you.

1. **Communication is Key:** Effective co-parenting begins with open and honest communication. Establish a method of communication that works for both parents, whether it's through email, text messaging,

or a co-parenting app. Consistent and respectful communication will help to avoid misunderstandings and conflicts.

2. **Define Roles and Responsibilities:** Clearly outline each parent's roles and responsibilities in the co-parenting plan. This includes decision-making responsibilities, visitation schedules, and financial obligations. By establishing clear boundaries, both parents can have a better understanding of their responsibilities and avoid unnecessary conflicts.

3. **Prioritise the Children's Well-being:** The Children's needs should be put in front of that of any parent. When creating a co-parenting plan, always prioritise the best interests of the children. Ensure that their physical, emotional, and psychological needs are met by considering their age, preferences, and any special circumstances. Collaborate if you can with the other parent to create a nurturing and stable environment for the children.

4. **Flexibility and Adaptability:** Recognise that flexibility is essential in a co-parenting plan. Life is unpredictable, and circumstances may change. Be open to revisiting and adjusting the plan as needed. A willingness to adapt will help create a harmonious co-parenting relationship.

5. **Conflict Resolution:** It's inevitable that conflicts may arise during the co-parenting journey. Establish

a process for resolving conflicts peacefully and constructively. Consider seeking the help of a mediator or therapist if necessary, as they can provide guidance and support in navigating difficult situations.

6. **Consistency and Routine:** Consistency is key in co-parenting. Establish a consistent routine and schedule that both parents can adhere to. This will provide stability and predictability for the children, helping them adjust to the new family dynamic.

Creating a co-parenting plan requires effort, compromise, and commitment from both parents. By focusing on effective communication, defining roles and responsibilities, prioritising the children's well-being, being flexible, resolving conflicts peacefully, and maintaining consistency, solo parents can create a nurturing and supportive co-parenting environment. Don't forget, the ultimate goal is to provide a loving and stable foundation for your children to thrive despite the challenges of divorce.

DEALING WITH CONFLICT AND DISAGREEMENTS

Conflict and disagreements are a natural part of any relationship, and single parenting is no exception. As a solo parent, you may find yourself facing numerous challenges and conflicts with your ex-spouse, your children, or even within yourself. However, it's important to remember that conflict does not have to be negative or destructive. With the right approach and mindset, conflicts can be an opportunity for growth, understanding, and ultimately, a healthier co-parenting dynamic.

One of the most influential ways of dealing with conflict and disagreements is effective communication. Clear and open communication can minimise misunderstandings and prevent conflicts from escalating. When discussing matters with your ex-spouse, try to remain calm, respectful, and focused on the issue at hand. Avoid blaming or attacking each other, as this can only worsen the situation. Instead, if its possible try to seek to understand each other's perspectives and find common ground for compromise.

It's also essential to prioritise the well-being of your children during conflicts. Shield them from any heated arguments or negative emotions between you and your ex-spouse. Remember that your children love both parents and should not be caught in the middle of your disagreements. Whenever possible, involve a mediator or seek professional help to resolve conflicts in a healthy and constructive manner.

Additionally, conflicts can arise within yourself as you navigate the challenges of parenting alone. It's normal to experience a range of emotions, such as anger, frustration, or sadness. Acknowledge and process these emotions, but also practice self-care and self-compassion. Seek support from friends, family, or a therapist who can provide guidance and help you maintain your emotional well-being.

Finally, conflicts and disagreements are not a reflection of your worth as a parent or as an individual. It's easy to feel overwhelmed or doubt your abilities during challenging times, but it's important to remind yourself that you're doing the best you can. Surround yourself with positive influences and affirmations to boost your self-confidence and remind yourself that you're capable of thriving as a solo parent.

So, to conclude, dealing with conflict and disagreements is an ongoing process in solo parenting. By practicing effective communication, prioritising your children's well-being, and taking care of yourself, you can navigate conflicts in a healthy and constructive way. Remember, conflicts can be opportunities for growth and understanding, leading to a more harmonious co-parenting relationship and ultimately, a thriving solo parenting journey.

Chapter 5

THRIVING FINANCIALLY AS A SOLO PARENT

BUDGETING AND FINANCIAL PLANNING

One of the most critical aspects of solo parenting is managing your finances effectively. As a solo parent, you're solely responsible for your children's well-being and ensuring financial stability for your family. Therefore, it's essential to develop a robust budgeting and financial planning strategy to navigate this new phase of life successfully.

Creating a budget is the foundation of sound financial management. Start by evaluating your income and expenses. Determine your fixed expenses, such as rent/mortgage, utilities, childcare, and insurance. Then, consider your variable expenses, such as groceries, transportation, entertainment, and extracurricular activities. It's very important to be realistic and honest with yourself about your income and expenses to avoid any unexpected financial troubles.

Once you have a clear picture of your financial situation, prioritise your expenses. Ensure that essential bills are paid first, followed by savings for emergencies and long-term goals. Consider setting up automatic transfers to a separate savings account to make saving easier and more consistent. Having an emergency fund will provide peace of mind during unexpected circumstances.

Additionally, it's crucial to create a plan for debt management. If you have outstanding debts from the divorce settlement or any other loans, develop a strategy to pay them off systematically. Allocate a portion of your budget to debt repayment and consider seeking professional advice if needed. Minimising debt will help you achieve financial stability in the long run.

As a solo parent, it's vital to prepare for the future by setting financial goals. Whether it's saving for your children's education, buying a home, or planning for retirement, having clear goals will guide your financial decisions. Break down these goals into manageable milestones and create a savings plan to achieve them gradually. Regularly revisit your goals and adjust your budget accordingly.

Lastly, don't forget the importance of self-care. Solo parenting can be emotionally and physically draining, and neglecting yourself can impact your financial well-being. Allocate a portion of your budget for self-care activities that help you relax and rejuvenate. Remember, taking care of yourself isn't a luxury but a necessity.

SEEKING CHILD SUPPORT AND SPOUSAL MAINTENANCE

Navigating the complexities of solo parenting after a divorce can be overwhelming, especially when it comes to financial matters. As a solo parent, you may find yourself in a situation where you need to seek child support and/or spousal maintenance to ensure the well-being of both yourself and your children. I'm now going to outline the importance of seeking child support, the processes involved and providing valuable tips to help you on this journey.

Child support serves as a crucial financial resource that can help you provide a stable and nurturing environment for your children. Child support ensures that your children's basic needs, such as food, clothing, education, and healthcare, are met. On the other hand, spousal support, provides financial assistance to the custodial parent to maintain a similar standard of living enjoyed during the marriage.

To seek child support and/or spousal maintenance effectively, it's essential to understand the legal process involved. Consulting with a family law solicitor who specialises in divorce and custody matters can provide you with the necessary guidance and support. They will help you gather the required documentation, such as financial statements, to present a strong case in court.

When seeking child support, it's vital to communicate openly and honestly with your ex-spouse. Presenting a clear and reasonable request can lead to a more amicable resolution, ultimately benefiting your children. However, if negotiations fail, be prepared to present your case in court, where a judge will determine the appropriate amount based on various factors, including income and the children's needs.

In the case of Spousal Maintenance, the court will consider factors such as the length of the marriage, each spouse's earning capacity, and the financial needs of both parties. It's imperative to present evidence of your financial situation, including income, expenses, and debts, to ensure a fair determination.

Seeking child support can provide your children with the best possible future. By seeking financial assistance, you're ensuring that your children's needs are met, allowing you to focus on creating a stable and loving environment for them.

Seeking child support and spousal maintenance is an essential step for solo parents after a divorce. By understanding the legal process, communicating effectively, and seeking the support of a Family law Solicitor, you can navigate this aspect of solo parenting with confidence. Remember, you're not alone in this journey, and by advocating for yourself and your children, you're taking a pivotal step towards confident parenting.

After going through a divorce, solo parents often find themselves facing new challenges, including the need to provide for their families single-handedly. One major aspect of this is finding job and career opportunities that can help them thrive in their new roles. This next section will guide solo parents through the process of exploring various employment options and building a fulfilling career path.

1. **Assessing Skills and Interests:** The first step in exploring job and career opportunities is to assess your skills, qualifications, and interests. Take the

time to reflect on your previous work experience, education, and any specialised skills you possess. Consider what you enjoy doing and what aligns with your personal values. This self-reflection will help you identify potential career paths that suit your unique circumstances and ambitions.

2. **Exploring Flexible Work Options:** Solo parents often face the challenge of balancing work and family responsibilities. It's essential to explore flexible work options that allow you to maintain a healthy work-life balance. Look for jobs that offer flexible hours or remote work arrangements. Additionally, consider freelancing or starting your own business to have more control over your schedule.

3. **Networking and Skill Development:** Building a strong professional network can be really beneficial for finding job opportunities and advancing in your career. Attend networking events, join relevant online communities, and connect with others in your field. Additionally, invest in skill development by attending workshops, online courses, or gaining certifications. Enhancing your skills will open doors to new job prospects and increase your marketability.

4. **Utilising Support Services:** Solo parents may face additional barriers when searching for employment, such as limited resources or childcare responsibilities. Take advantage of support services provided by local organisations or community programs. These services

may include job coaching, resume writing assistance, or financial aid programs. Seek out resources specifically tailored to solo parents, as they can provide invaluable support during your job search.

5. **Long-term Career Planning:** While immediate employment is a major factor, it's equally important to consider long-term career planning. Set goals for yourself and create a roadmap to reach them. Consider the potential for growth and advancement in your chosen field. Explore opportunities for further education or professional development to enhance your career prospects over time.

By exploring job and career opportunities, you can regain financial independence while building a fulfilling career.

Keep in mind, this journey may have its ups and downs, but by assessing your skills, exploring flexible work options, networking, utilising support services, and planning for the long term, you *can* pave a path towards a successful and rewarding professional life.

Chapter 6

NURTURING YOUR CHILDREN'S WELL-BEING

SUPPORTING THEIR EMOTIONAL NEEDS

As a solo parent navigating the challenging terrain of post-divorce life, it's crucial to prioritise the emotional well-being of your children. This chapter delves into the importance of supporting your emotional needs and offers practical strategies to help you become a nurturing and empathetic parent during this transitional period.

Divorce can be an emotionally tumultuous experience for children, leaving them feeling confused, anxious, and even guilty. It's *essential* to create a safe and supportive environment where they can freely express their emotions without fear of judgment. Encourage open communication by setting aside dedicated time for family discussions, where each member can share their thoughts and feelings. Active listening is critical here, as it helps your children feel heard and validated.

Additionally, it's vital to be aware of any changes in your children's behaviour or mood. Divorce can often lead to feelings of sadness, anger, or withdrawal. Stay attuned to these signs and offer your children the space they need to process their emotions. Encourage them to share their feelings, whether through talking, writing, or engaging in creative outlets such as art or music.

Building a strong support network for both yourself and your children is another key aspect of meeting their emotional needs. Seek out other solo parents or divorce support groups in your community where you can connect with individuals facing similar challenges. Engaging in these communities can provide a safe space for sharing experiences, gaining advice, and finding solace.

Another effective way to support your children's emotional needs is by maintaining consistent routines and boundaries. Divorce often disrupts the stability children crave, so establishing regular family rituals can help provide a sense of security and normalcy. Encourage healthy habits like regular exercise, a balanced diet, and sufficient sleep, as these contribute to emotional well-being.

Lastly, make self-care a priority (I know I keep repeating this in the book but it's SO important) As a solo parent, it's easy to neglect your own emotional needs while focusing on your children's well-being. However, taking care of yourself ultimately allows you to be a better parent. Make time for activities that bring you joy, whether it's pursuing a hobby, spending time with friends, or seeking therapy if needed. Dont forget, *your* emotional well-being is directly linked to that of your children.

Supporting your children's emotional needs is an essential aspect of parenting, especially when you're doing it alone. By creating a safe and open environment, being attuned to their emotions, building a support network, establishing routines, and practicing self-care, you can help your children navigate the emotional challenges of divorce and thrive as resilient individuals.

CO-PARENTING DISCIPLINE STRATEGIES

Discipline is an essential aspect of parenting, and when it comes to co-parenting after a divorce, it becomes even more important. As a single parent, you may face unique challenges in maintaining discipline while navigating the complexities of co-parenting. The following tips will explore effective discipline strategies specifically tailored for single parents.

1. **Consistency is key:** Consistency is vital in co-parenting discipline. Establish consistent rules and consequences between both households to ensure your child has a clear understanding of expectations regardless of where they are. Regular communication with your ex-spouse about discipline matters can help maintain consistency and avoid confusion.

2. **Unified front:** While co-parenting, it's important to present a united front to your child. Avoid undermining each other's authority or disciplining methods in front of the child. Instead, discuss any disagreements privately and present a united front when addressing discipline issues with your child.

3. **Set clear boundaries:** Clearly define boundaries and rules for your child, taking into account their age, maturity, and individual needs. Communicate these rules to your child and ensure they understand them. Consistently reinforcing these boundaries will help your child develop a sense of structure and discipline.

4. **Positive reinforcement:** Focus on positive reinforcement rather than solely relying on punishment. Praise and rewards for good behaviour can be powerful motivators for children. Acknowledge and appreciate your child's efforts, and celebrate their achievements to encourage positive behaviour.

5. **Effective communication:** Open and effective communication with your child is vital in co-parenting discipline. Listen to their concerns, explain the reasons behind rules, and encourage them to express their feelings. By fostering open dialogue, you can better understand their perspective and address any disciplinary issues effectively.

6. **Flexibility and adaptation:** Co-parenting after a divorce requires flexibility and adaptation. Be open to adjusting discipline strategies as your child grows and their needs change. What may have worked when they were younger might not be effective as they enter adolescence. Stay attuned to their developmental stages and adapt your discipline methods accordingly.

7. **Seek professional help if needed:** If you find yourself struggling with co-parenting discipline issues, don't

hesitate to seek professional help. Family therapists or counsellors can provide guidance and support to help you navigate the challenges of co-parenting.

By implementing these co-parenting discipline strategies, you can create a stable and nurturing environment for your child. Co-parenting requires cooperation and compromise, but with consistent discipline strategies, you can help your child thrive despite the challenges they may face.

FACILITATING HEALTHY RELATIONSHIPS WITH THE OTHER PARENT

One of the most pivotal aspects of solo parenting after a divorce is establishing and maintaining a healthy relationship with the other parent if you can. While it may feel daunting or even impossible at times, fostering a positive co-parenting dynamic can greatly benefit both you and your children in the long run. Let me share some essential strategies and tools to facilitate healthy relationships with the other parent. It's understandable that in some marriage breakdowns, this will not be possible.

1. **Communication is key:** Effective communication is the foundation of *any successful co-parenting relationship.* Regularly discuss parenting matters, schedules, and any concerns that arise. Be open, respectful, and focused on the best interests of your children. Use various mediums such as phone calls, emails, or even co-parenting apps to ensure clear and consistent communication.

2. **Set boundaries and expectations:** It's essential to establish boundaries and expectations early on to avoid conflicts and confusion. Discuss and agree on parenting styles, discipline strategies, and rules for consistency across both households. Clearly define custody and visitation schedules, holidays, and special occasions to ensure everyone is on the same page.
3. **Prioritise the children's well-being:** Your children's happiness and well-being should *always* be the top priority. Encourage a healthy and loving relationship between the children and the other parent. Avoid speaking negatively about the other parent, as it can be harmful to the children's emotional development. Focus on fostering an environment where your children feel loved and supported by both parents. The Children's needs should always come before the parents needs.
4. **Be flexible and considerate:** Flexibility is crucial in co-parenting. Life is unpredictable, and unexpected events may arise that require adjustments to schedules or plans. Show understanding and be willing to accommodate changes when necessary. This will foster goodwill and cooperation between both parents.
5. **Seek professional guidance if needed:** Co-parenting can be challenging, especially when conflicts persist or emotions run high. Don't hesitate to seek professional help, such as therapy or mediation, to assist in resolving disputes or improving communication. These

resources can provide valuable strategies and tools to overcome obstacles and create a more supportive co-parenting relationship.

Facilitating a healthy relationship with the other parent takes time, patience, and effort. By prioritising open communication, setting boundaries, and focusing on the well-being of your children, you can create a positive co-parenting dynamic that allows your family to thrive post-divorce.

Chapter 7

CREATING A HAPPY AND STABLE HOME ENVIRONMENT

ESTABLISHING ROUTINES AND STRUCTURES

In the turbulent aftermath of a divorce, solo parents face the daunting task of re-establishing stability and structure in their lives. This chapter explores into the importance of establishing routines and structures to help you succeed as a single parent.

After the upheaval of a divorce, it's imperative to create a sense of normality and predictability for both yourself and your children. Routines provide a framework that helps establish a sense of security and stability in an otherwise uncertain time. They also help children adapt to the changes in their lives more easily. By setting regular meal times, bedtimes, and daily activities, you can create a reliable and consistent environment for your children, fostering a sense of comfort and reducing anxiety.

One effective way to establish routines is by creating a daily schedule. Start by outlining the major activities that need to take place each day, such as meals, school drop-offs, work commitments, and extracurricular activities. Then, build in designated times for household chores, self-care, and quality time with your children. Be sure to communicate the schedule clearly with your children, so they know what to expect and can actively participate in following it.

Structures, on the other hand, refer to the rules and boundaries that you set within your household. Establishing clear guidelines for behaviour, chores, and responsibilities will help maintain harmony and order. Clearly communicate these expectations to your children, ensuring they understand the consequences of breaking the rules. Consistency is key here, as it will help your children feel safe and secure in their new family dynamic.

It's also important to remember that routines and structures should not stifle individuality or flexibility. Allow room for spontaneity and adaptability within the established framework. Flexibility is especially important when co-parenting with your ex-spouse, as it can help navigate the complexities of shared custody or visitation arrangements.

By establishing routines and structures, you're not only creating a stable environment for your children but also laying the foundation for their emotional well-being and success. As a solo parent, it may feel overwhelming at times, but remember that you're not alone. Connect with support groups, seek professional help when needed, and have open and honest communication with your children. With time, patience, and dedication, you can create a brilliant life for yourself and your children.

MANAGING HOUSEHOLD RESPONSIBILITIES

As a solo parent, managing household responsibilities can often feel overwhelming. With the weight of raising children on your shoulders, it's essential to develop effective strategies to ensure that your home runs smoothly and efficiently. Here are some practical tips and empowering insights on how to manage household responsibilities.

1. **Establish a Routine:** Creating a daily routine for yourself and your children can bring structure and stability to your household. Set specific times for meals, chores, homework, and downtime. This routine will not only help you manage your time effectively but also provide a sense of predictability for your children.

2. **Delegate Tasks:** Remember that you don't have to do everything on your own. Depending on the age of your children, assign age-appropriate tasks to help with household chores. This not only lightens your load but also teaches your children the importance of responsibility and teamwork.

3. **Simplify Your Home:** Clutter can add unnecessary stress to an already busy life. Take the time to declutter and organise your home. Create designated spaces for toys, school supplies, and other essential items. This will make it easier for you and your children to find what you need and maintain a clean living environment.

4. **Prioritise Self-Care:** It's vital to prioritise self-care as a solo parent. Taking care of yourself physically, mentally, and emotionally will enable you to better manage your household responsibilities. Set aside time for activities that rejuvenate you, such as exercise, hobbies, or spending time with friends.

5. **Seek Support:** Don't hesitate to reach out for support when needed. Connect with other solo parents in your community or join support groups. Sharing experiences and advice can be immensely helpful in navigating the challenges of solo parenting.

6. **Teach Life Skills:** As a solo parent, it's crucial to equip your children with essential life skills. Teach them how to do laundry, cook simple meals, manage finances, and other practical tasks. By involving them in household responsibilities, you not only lighten your load but also prepare them for independent living in the future.

Managing household responsibilities as a solo parent may be challenging at times, but with the right strategies and mindset, you can create a thriving and harmonious home.

By establishing routines, delegating tasks, simplifying your living space, prioritising self-care, seeking support, and teaching life skills, you will not only manage your household effectively but also create a nurturing environment for you and your children.

PROMOTING A POSITIVE AND SUPPORTIVE ATMOSPHERE

As a solo parent navigating the challenging journey of parenting, creating a positive and supportive atmosphere for both yourself and your children becomes crucial. The aftermath of divorce can be emotionally taxing and overwhelming, but with the right mindset and strategies, you can foster a healthy and nurturing environment for your family to thrive. Let's explore some practical tips and techniques to promote a positive and supportive atmosphere in your solo parenting journey.

First and foremost, Look after your own wellbeing. Remember that you cannot pour from an empty cup. Taking care of your physical, mental, and emotional health will enable you to be a more present and supportive parent. Set aside time for activities that bring you joy and help you recharge, whether it's engaging in a hobby, exercising, or simply enjoying a quiet moment alone. By investing in yourself, you will be better equipped to handle the challenges of solo parenting and create a positive atmosphere for your children.

Communication is another vital aspect of promoting a positive environment. Encourage open and honest dialogue with your children, allowing them to express their feelings, concerns, and fears. Ensure that your children know they can come to you for support and that their emotions are valid. Active listening and empathy play a significant role in making your child feel heard and understood.

In addition to fostering open communication, consistency and routine are crucial for a stable and supportive atmosphere. Establishing a predictable schedule can provide a sense of security and structure for your children, helping them adjust to their new reality. Consistency also helps build trust and reliability, which are essential for a positive parent-child relationship.

Promoting a positive atmosphere also involves setting boundaries and expectations. Establish clear rules and guidelines for behavior and ensure they are consistently enforced. By setting boundaries, you create a safe and predictable environment that promotes healthy development and respect.

Lastly, seek out a support network of fellow solo parents who understand your unique challenges and can provide guidance, empathy, and practical advice. Connect with local support groups or online communities to share experiences, seek help, and gain a sense of belonging. Surrounding yourself and your children with a supportive community can make a world of difference in promoting a positive and nurturing atmosphere.

Promoting a positive and supportive atmosphere as a solo parent requires self-care, open communication, consistency, boundaries, and a supportive network. By implementing these strategies, you can foster a safe and nurturing environment where both you and your children can thrive and find happiness amid the challenges of solo parenting.

Chapter 8

BALANCING WORK AND PARENTING

EXPLORING FLEXIBLE WORK OPTIONS

One of the biggest challenges faced by solo parents is finding the right work-life balance. Juggling the responsibilities of parenting, managing a household, and pursuing a career can often feel overwhelming. However, there is a solution – exploring flexible work options.

Flexible work arrangements can provide solo parents with the freedom and flexibility they need to successfully navigate the demands of their new life. These arrangements allow parents to have more control over their schedules, enabling them to prioritise their parenting duties while still maintaining a fulfilling career.

One popular flexible work option is remote work. Thanks to advancements in technology, many professions can now be carried out from the comfort of home. Solo parents can leverage this opportunity to create a workspace that accommodates their unique needs. By working remotely, they can eliminate the stress of commuting, save time, and have the freedom to be present for their children's important moments.

Another flexible work option to consider is part-time employment. Transitioning from a traditional full-time job to part-time work can offer solo parents a better work-life balance. It allows them to devote more time to their children while still earning an income. Part-time work can also provide the opportunity to explore new career paths or pursue personal interests.

Freelancing or starting a home-based business is another flexible work option worth exploring. Solo parents can leverage their skills and expertise to offer services or create products from the comfort of their own home. This option allows for greater control over working hours and the freedom to choose projects that align with their lifestyle.

Additionally, job sharing or flexible scheduling can be negotiated with employers. By discussing the possibility of reduced hours or alternative work arrangements, solo parents can create a tailored work schedule that meets both their professional and personal needs.

When exploring flexible work options, it's essential for solo parents to consider their financial situation and the potential impact on their career trajectory. It may be helpful to seek guidance from career counsellorss or financial advisors to ensure the chosen path aligns with long-term goals.

Exploring flexible work options can be a game-changer for solo parents navigating the challenges of parenting. Remote work, part-time employment, freelancing, or negotiating flexible schedules can all provide the freedom and flexibility needed to thrive as a solo parent. By finding the right work-life balance, solo parents can create a fulfilling life for themselves and their children while successfully pursuing their career aspirations.

MANAGING TIME AND PRIORITIES

As a solo parent navigating life after divorce, one of the most valuable skills you can develop is effective time management. Balancing your responsibilities as a parent, a provider, and an individual can often feel overwhelming, but with the right strategies, you can regain control of your time and priorities.

1. **Set Clear Priorities:** Begin by identifying your top priorities and values in life. This will help you align your activities with what truly matters to you and your children. Make a list of your daily, weekly, and monthly tasks, and rank them based on importance. Focus on the top priorities and delegate or eliminate non-essential tasks to create more time for what truly matters.

2. **Establish a Routine:** Creating a consistent daily routine can provide structure and stability for both you and your children. Set regular wake-up and bedtimes, meal times, and designated time for work, household chores, and quality time with your children. A routine helps minimise decision fatigue and ensures that essential tasks are completed regularly.

3. **Delegate and Seek Support:** Don't be afraid to ask for help or delegate tasks to others. Reach out to family members, friends, or neighbours who may be willing

to assist with childcare, running errands, or household chores. Consider joining support groups or online communities for solo parents to share advice, resources, and support.

4. **Practice Effective Time Blocking:** Time blocking involves scheduling specific blocks of time for different activities. Dedicate uninterrupted periods for work, household chores, quality time with your children, self-care, and personal interests. Use digital calendars, planners, or apps to organise and visualise your daily schedule.

5. **Learn to Say No:** As a solo parent, your time and energy are limited resources. Be mindful of taking on too many commitments and learn to say no when necessary. Avoid overextending yourself to prevent burnout.

6. **Utilise Technology and Automation:** Take advantage of technology and automation tools to streamline your tasks. Use online grocery shopping, meal delivery services, or home cleaning services to save time. Explore productivity apps that can help you manage your to-do lists, set reminders, and stay organised.

Managing time and priorities is an ongoing process. Be flexible and willing to adjust your schedule as needed while keeping your priorities in focus. By mastering these skills, you can create a balanced and fulfilling life for you and your children.

SEEKING CHILDCARE SOLUTIONS

As a solo parent navigating the challenging terrain of post-divorce life, one of the most critical aspects to consider is finding reliable and suitable childcare solutions. Balancing work, personal commitments, and the responsibilities of raising children on your own can be overwhelming, but with the right strategies, you can handle it all with grace and confidence.

1. **Evaluate Your Needs:** Assessing your specific childcare requirements is the first step towards finding the best solution. Consider factors such as your work schedule, your children's age and needs, and any additional support systems you may have. This evaluation will help you determine the type of childcare that suits your family's unique circumstances.

2. **Explore Daycare Options:** Nurseries are a popular choice for many solo parents. They offer a structured environment where your child can learn, play, and socialise with other children. Research local daycare Nurseries/crèche, visit them, and consider factors such as their proximity to your home or workplace, their reputation, and the qualifications and experience of the caregivers.

3. **Look into In-Home Care:** Another viable option for solo parents is hiring a nanny or au pair to provide care in the comfort of your own home. This arrangement offers flexibility and may be particularly beneficial if your work schedule is irregular or if you have multiple

children with different needs. Ensure you thoroughly vet potential candidates, check references, and conduct interviews to ensure a good fit. Or a local Childminder who would have the registration, qualifications and safeguarding requirements to look after your child.

4. **Co-Parenting and Shared Care:** If possible, explore the option of co-parenting or shared care with your ex-spouse. While this arrangement may not be suitable for all situations, it can provide stability and consistency for your children while alleviating some of the childcare burden on you. Open and honest communication with your ex-spouse is crucial to ensure a harmonious co-parenting relationship.

5. **Engage Family and Friends:** Reach out to your extended family, friends, and support network for assistance with childcare. Grandparents, siblings, or close friends may be able to help out during times when you need extra support. Establish clear communication and boundaries to ensure that everyone involved understands their role and responsibilities.

Seeking childcare solutions as a solo parent is a testament to your dedication to your children's well-being. Take the time to explore different options, consider your unique circumstances, and choose the solution that aligns best with your family's needs. With the right support and a solid childcare plan in place, you can confidently navigate the difficulties of solo parenting and create a harmonious environment for both you and your children.

Chapter 9

MOVING FORWARD AND EMBRACING SINGLE PARENTHOOD

EMBRACING YOUR NEW IDENTITY

After going through the challenging process of divorce, solo parenting can feel like an overwhelming responsibility. However, it's crucial to remember that you're not alone in this journey. In this Chapter, I'll outline the concept of embracing your new identity as a solo parent and provide valuable insights and tips for navigating this phase successfully.

Firstly, it's essential to acknowledge that your identity has undergone a significant transformation. You're no longer defined solely by your role as a spouse, but as a resilient and capable solo parent. Embracing this new identity is a key step towards finding empowerment and embracing your newfound independence.

One important aspect of embracing your new identity is learning to *let go* of any guilt or self-blame associated with the divorce. Recognise that divorce is a complex and multifaceted process, and it's not solely your responsibility. Sometimes it can be due to reasons such as Infidelity, Abuse, and many more, some circumstances when divorce takes place may be out of your control. Try to be present and emotionally available to your children, everyone is going through a process of change.

Another important element of embracing your new identity is building a support network. Reach out to other solo parents who have gone through similar experiences. Join local support groups or online communities that provide a safe space for sharing stories, advice, and encouragement. Surrounding yourself with people who understand your unique challenges can provide a sense of belonging and alleviate feelings of isolation. Meet up with your friends old and new, Take up a new hobby.

It's also important to set realistic expectations for yourself and your children. Solo parenting comes with its own set of challenges and limitations. Understand that you cannot do everything alone, and it's okay to ask for help when needed. Delegating tasks, seeking assistance from family and friends, or even hiring professional help can alleviate some of the burdens and allow you to focus on being the best parent you can be.

Finally, take some time to rediscover your own passions and interests. Embracing your new identity does not mean sacrificing your own happiness. Pursue activities that bring you joy and allow you to recharge. Engaging in self-care will not only benefit you but also set an excellent example for your children.

SETTING GOALS AND CREATING A VISION FOR THE FUTURE

Embracing your new identity as a solo parent is a transformative process that requires patience, self-compassion, and a supportive network. By letting go of guilt, building a support system, setting realistic expectations, and prioritising self-care, you will not only thrive as a solo parent but also create a nurturing environment for your children to grow and flourish. Embrace this new chapter of your life with confidence and resilience, and remember that you're capable of creating a fulfilling and joyful future for yourself and your children.

> As a solo parent navigating the challenging terrain of post-divorce life, it's vital to set goals and create a vision for the future.

Setting goals allows you to have a roadmap for your life, providing direction and purpose. It's important to set both short-term and long-term goals that align with your values and aspirations. Start by identifying what is most important to you and what you want to achieve in different areas of your life – be it your career, parenting, personal development, or relationships.

When setting goals, it's essential to be realistic and specific. Break down your long-term goals into smaller, manageable steps that you can work towards in the short term. This way, you can track your progress and celebrate your achievements along the way, boosting your motivation and confidence.

Creating a vision for the future is equally important. Picture the life you want to build for yourself and your children. Visualise the kind of parent you aspire to be and the type of environment you want to create for your family. This vision will serve as a guiding light during challenging times and help you make decisions that align with your desired future.

To create a vision, take time to reflect on your values and priorities. What kind of parent do you want to be? What values do you want to instill in your children? What activities or experiences do you want to share with them? Having a clear vision will not only help you stay focused but also serve as a source of inspiration and motivation.

Remember, setting goals and creating a vision is an ongoing process. Review and revise your goals regularly as circumstances change and new opportunities arise. As you achieve your goals, set new ones that challenge and excite you. Allow your vision to evolve as you grow and learn as a solo parent.

> By setting goals and creating a vision for the future, you're taking proactive steps towards creating the life you desire. Embrace this opportunity to build a fulfilling and thriving life for yourself and your children.

FINDING JOY AND HAPPINESS IN SOLO PARENTING

Solo parenting can be a challenging and overwhelming journey, but it's also an opportunity for personal growth, self-discovery, and finding joy and happiness in unexpected places. Here are some various strategies and mindsets that can help solo parents navigate this new chapter of their lives with optimism and fulfillment.

It's essential to acknowledge and accept your emotions. Divorce often brings a range of emotions like grief, anger, and disappointment. It's necessary to give yourself permission to feel these emotions and process them in a healthy way. By acknowledging your feelings and seeking support from friends, family, or a therapist, you can begin the healing process and create space for joy and happiness to enter your life.

One key aspect of finding joy and happiness is learning to embrace your independence. Now that you are a solo parent, you have the opportunity to rediscover yourself and establish a new sense of identity. Take advantage of this chance to pursue your passions, hobbies, and interests. Explore new activities, join clubs or groups that align with your interests, and dedicate time to self-care. By nurturing your own happiness, you will become a more fulfilled and joyful parent.

Another essential element of finding joy in solo parenting is building a support system. Surround yourself with people who uplift and empower you. Seek out other solo parents who can relate to your experiences and provide a listening ear. Join support groups or online communities where you can share your triumphs and challenges. By connecting with others who have walked a similar path, you will find solace, encouragement, and practical advice.

Furthermore, practicing gratitude can significantly impact your overall well-being and happiness. Each day, take a moment to reflect on the things you are grateful for, no matter how small they may seem. Appreciating the love and joy your children bring into your life, the support of your friends and family, or even the beauty of nature can help shift your focus from the difficulties of solo parenting to the blessings that surround you.

Lastly, remember to be gentle with yourself. Parenting isn't an easy task, and you may face setbacks along the way. Embrace imperfection and celebrate small victories. Give yourself credit for the incredible strength and resilience you demonstrate every day. By practicing self-compassion, you will cultivate a sense of inner peace and contentment.

To conclude; solo parenting can be a challenging journey, but it also presents an opportunity for growth and happiness. By acknowledging and processing your emotions, embracing your independence, building a support system, practicing gratitude, and being gentle with yourself, you can find joy and happiness in solo parenting. With the right mindset and support, you can thrive as a solo parent.

Chapter 10

CO-PARENTING CHALLENGES AND SOLUTIONS

DEALING WITH DIFFICULT EX-PARTNERS

One of the most challenging aspects of single parenting is learning how to deal with difficult ex-partners. Co-parenting can be a complex and often emotional journey, but with the right strategies and mindset, it's possible to navigate these difficulties and create a harmonious environment for both you and your children. In this section, we will explore effective ways to handle the challenges that arise from dealing with difficult ex-partners.

Firstly, it's essential to prioritise communication. Open and healthy communication is the key to successful co-parenting. Set aside any personal grievances or emotions and focus solely on the needs and best interests of your children. Keep conversations concise, clear, and respectful. If face-to-face interactions are too challenging, consider using alternative communication methods such as email or text messaging.

Another vital aspect of dealing with difficult ex-partners is setting boundaries. Establish clear boundaries and expectations regarding parenting responsibilities, schedules, and decision-making. Clearly define each parent's role and stick to the agreed-upon arrangements. By maintaining consistent boundaries, you can minimise conflicts and create a sense of stability for your children.

It's also crucial to separate your emotions from your interactions with your ex-partner. It's natural to experience a range of emotions after a divorce, but allowing these emotions to impact your co-parenting relationship can be detrimental. Seek support from friends, family, or a therapist to process your emotions separately from your interactions with your ex-partner. By doing so, you can approach co-parenting with a clear and level-headed mindset.

In some cases, professional mediation or counselling may be necessary. If communication and cooperation with your ex-partner become extremely difficult or strained, seeking professional help can be beneficial. A mediator or therapist can provide guidance, facilitate productive discussions, and help both parties find common ground.

Lastly, remember to prioritise self-care. Solo parenting can be emotionally and physically draining. Take time for yourself to recharge and engage in activities that bring you joy and relaxation. By taking care of your own well-being, you can better handle the challenges that come with dealing with a difficult ex-partner.

Dealing with difficult ex-partners is undoubtedly a challenging aspect. However, with effective communication, clear boundaries, emotional separation, and self-care, it Can be possible to navigate these difficulties and create a positive co-parenting environment for both you and your children. Understandably though it needs both parents to be on board with this and more often than not one of the parents will not wish to co -parent. Remember this is no reflection on you but on them. The well-being and happiness of your children should always be the ultimate goal.

HANDLING PARENTAL ALIENATION

Parental alienation is a significant challenge that many divorced parents face. It refers to the deliberate actions of one parent to distance the child from the other parent, often resulting in strained relationships and emotional distress for all parties involved. Here are some effective strategies for handling parental alienation and fostering a healthy relationship with your child.

1. **Recognise the signs:** Parental alienation can manifest in various ways, such as negative comments about the other parent, limiting communication or visitation, or even false accusations. Being aware of these signs is crucial in addressing the issue promptly.

2. **Promote open communication:** Establish an open line of communication with your child, emphasising that they can freely express their thoughts and feelings about the other parent without fear of judgment. Encourage them to share their experiences and actively listen to their concerns.

3. **Focus on the child's well-being:** Your child's well-being should *always* be the top priority. Avoid engaging in negative discussions about the other parent or using them as a pawn in conflicts. Instead, maintain a positive attitude and provide a safe and supportive environment for your child.

4. **Seek professional help**: If parental alienation persists and negatively impacts your child's mental and emotional health, consider seeking professional help. A therapist or counsellor experienced in family matters can provide guidance and support to navigate this challenging situation.

5. **Document incidents:** Keep a record of any incidents involving parental alienation, including dates, times, and specific actions taken. This documentation can serve as evidence if legal intervention becomes necessary.

6. **Educate yourself:** Gain a thorough understanding of parental alienation and its effects. Read books, attend seminars, or join support groups focused on solo parenting. The more knowledge you have, the better equipped you will be to handle the situation.

7. **Involve legal professionals if needed:** In severe cases of parental alienation, involving legal professionals may be necessary. Consult with a family law attorney who specialises in child custody matters to explore your options and protect your child's rights.

Remember, handling parental alienation requires patience, resilience, and a focus on promoting the well-being of your child. By taking proactive steps, seeking support, and maintaining a positive outlook, you can work towards building a healthy relationship with your child.

RESOLVING CO-PARENTING CONFLICTS IN A HEALTHY WAY

Co-parenting after a divorce can be a daunting task, filled with its own unique set of challenges. As a single parent, it's essential to navigate these conflicts in a healthy and constructive manner for the well-being of both yourself and your children. Let's now look at effective strategies to resolve co-parenting conflicts and foster a positive co-parenting relationship.

> Communication is *key*. Establishing open and honest lines of communication with your ex-spouse plays a large part in creating a healthy co-parenting dynamic.

Set aside any animosity or negative emotions and focus on the well-being of your children. Practice active listening and empathy, allowing both parties to express their concerns and perspectives without interruption or judgment. By maintaining a respectful and cooperative attitude, you can work together to find mutually agreeable solutions.

Another important aspect of resolving co-parenting conflicts is maintaining boundaries. Clearly define your roles and responsibilities as co-parents and respect each other's boundaries. Avoid engaging in confrontations or power struggles, as this can negatively impact your children and lead to increased tension. Instead, strive for compromise and find common ground, always keeping the best interests of your children at the forefront.

It's also beneficial to establish a structured co-parenting plan. This plan should outline important details such as visitation schedules, holidays, and decision-making processes. By having a well-defined plan in place, you can reduce ambiguity and minimise potential conflicts. Regularly review and update the plan as needed, taking into account the changing needs and circumstances of your children and yourselves.

Seeking professional help can also be immensely beneficial in resolving co-parenting conflicts. Consider attending mediation sessions or engaging in family therapy to gain guidance and support from impartial experts. These professionals can provide valuable insights and strategies to navigate conflicts effectively and promote healthy communication.

Single parenting can be emotionally draining, and it's essential to take care of yourself. Engage in activities that bring you joy and help you recharge. Reach out to support networks, such as friends, family, or support groups specifically designed for solo parents. Remember, a healthy and happy parent is better equipped to handle co-parenting conflicts and provide a nurturing environment for their children.

Resolving co-parenting conflicts in a healthy way is vital to the well-being of both solo parents and their children. By fostering open communication, establishing boundaries, utilising a structured co-parenting plan, seeking professional help, and prioritising self-care, solo parents can navigate these conflicts with grace and create a positive co-parenting relationship that benefits everyone involved.

Chapter 11

HELPING YOUR CHILDREN ADJUST AND THRIVE

SUPPORTING THEIR EMOTIONAL HEALING

Divorce can be an emotionally challenging experience for everyone involved, especially for solo parents who are left to navigate the aftermath on their own. As a solo parent, it's crucial to prioritise not only your own emotional healing but also that of your children. Let's now delve into effective strategies and techniques to support your children's emotional healing.

Firstly, it's essential to create a safe and open environment for your children to express their feelings. Encourage open communication and let them know that their emotions are valid. Be an active listener and provide a judgment-free space for them to share their thoughts, fears, and concerns. By doing so, you're helping them process their emotions and fostering a sense of trust and security.

One effective way to support your children's emotional healing is by involving them in decision-making processes. Allow them to have a say in matters that directly affect them, such as visitation schedules or living arrangements. This involvement empowers them, boosts their self-esteem, and helps them feel more in control during a time of uncertainty.

It's also crucial to establish consistent routines and provide stability in their lives. Divorce often disrupts the familiar structure of a family, and children may feel overwhelmed by the changes. By maintaining regular schedules and routines, you're providing a sense of stability and normalcy, which can greatly contribute to their emotional well-being.

Additionally, consider seeking professional help if necessary. Therapy can be a valuable resource for your children to process their emotions and develop healthy coping mechanisms. A qualified therapist can guide them through the healing process and provide them with the tools they need to navigate the challenges of divorce.

As a solo parent, it's essential to take care of yourself and model healthy coping strategies. Children learn by observing their parents, so it's really important to show them how to handle difficult emotions in a positive way. Engage in activities that bring you joy and relaxation. By taking care of yourself, you're better equipped to support your children's emotional healing.

Supporting your children's emotional healing after divorce is a process that requires patience, empathy, and open communication. By creating a safe environment, involving them in decision-making, providing stability, seeking professional help when needed, and modelling healthy coping strategies, you can help your children thrive in the face of adversity. With the right support and guidance, both you and your children can heal and thrive together.

PROVIDING STABILITY AND CONSISTENCY

In the aftermath of a divorce, the challenges of single parenting can often feel overwhelming. As a solo parent, you may find yourself juggling multiple responsibilities, emotions, and uncertainties on a daily basis. However, by focusing on providing stability and consistency for yourself and your children, you can create a nurturing environment that promotes growth and resilience. Below are the essential strategies to help you maintain stability and consistency in your parenting journey.

Establishing a Routine

One of the most effective ways to provide stability for your children is by establishing a consistent daily routine. Children thrive on predictability and knowing what to expect, especially during times of change. Design a schedule that includes consistent wake-up and bedtimes, meal times, homework or study periods, and recreational activities. By adhering to a routine, you create a sense of structure and security that will help your children feel more grounded and stable.

Communication is Key

Maintaining open lines of communication with your children is paramount. Encourage them to express their thoughts, concerns, and emotions freely. Provide a safe space where they can talk about their experiences and ask questions. Regularly check in with them individually and as a family to address any issues that may arise. Clear and consistent communication will help foster trust and a sense of stability within your family unit.

Co-parenting Collaboration

If possible, strive for effective co-parenting with your ex-spouse. Collaborating on parenting decisions and maintaining consistent rules and expectations across households can greatly benefit your children. Openly discuss important matters, such as discipline, education, and healthcare, to minimise confusion and provide a stable environment for your children.

Self-Care and Emotional Stability

Take time for yourself to recharge and process your own emotions. Seek support from friends, family members, or support groups who understand the challenges you face. By looking after your own well-being, you will be better equipped to provide stability and consistency for your children.

To summarise, solo parenting after divorce is undoubtedly a challenging journey, but by focusing on providing stability and consistency, you can create a nurturing environment for your children to thrive. Establishing routines, maintaining open communication, collaborating with your ex-spouse, and prioritising self-care are essential strategies that will contribute to the stability and well-being of your family. Remember, you're not alone in this journey, and by implementing these strategies, you can navigate the challenges of solo parenting with resilience and create a bright future for yourself and your children.

ENCOURAGING THEIR GROWTH AND INDEPENDENCE

One of your primary goals is to encourage the growth and independence of your children. While the journey may be challenging at times, fostering their development in a nurturing and supportive environment is fundamental for their overall well-being and future success.

Firstly, it's essential to establish open lines of communication with your children. Encourage them to express their thoughts, feelings, and concerns, and listen to them attentively. By providing a safe space for them to share their emotions, you're helping them develop essential communication skills and emotional intelligence. This will not only strengthen your bond but also contribute to their overall growth and independence.

Another vital aspect of encouraging their growth and independence is to empower your children to make decisions and take responsibility for their actions. Allow them to have a say in age-appropriate matters, such as choosing their extracurricular activities or deciding how to spend their free time. By involving them in decision-making processes, you're providing them with valuable life skills, boosting their confidence, and nurturing their independence.

It's equally important to support your children's interests and hobbies. Encourage them to explore their passions and provide the necessary resources and opportunities for them to pursue their interests. Whether it's enrolling them in music lessons, sports teams, or art classes, supporting their hobbies will not only help them develop their talents but also instill a sense of self-confidence and independence.

Furthermore, it's vital to set clear boundaries and expectations for your children. Establishing consistent rules and routines provides them with a sense of stability and structure, which are essential for their growth and development. By setting appropriate boundaries, you're teaching them self-discipline, respect, and responsibility, all of which are transferable skills for leading independent lives.

Finally, encourage your children to embrace challenges and learn from their mistakes. Teach them that setbacks and failures are part of life and that they should view them as opportunities for growth and self-improvement. By fostering a growth mindset, you're equipping them with resilience and the ability to overcome obstacles, which are invaluable qualities for their future success.

To recap, encouraging the growth and independence of your children is a *fundamental*. Through effective communication, empowering decision-making, supporting their interests, setting boundaries, and fostering resilience, you can provide them with the tools they need to thrive independently. Remember, your role as a solo parent isn't just to provide love and support, but also to guide them towards becoming confident, independent individuals capable of navigating life's challenges with grace.

Chapter 12

OVERCOMING LONELINESS AND FINDING CONNECTION

COMBATING FEELINGS OF ISOLATION

One of the most challenging aspects of solo parenting after a divorce is the overwhelming feeling of isolation. As a solo parent, it's common to experience a sense of loneliness and disconnection from the outside world. There are countless solo parents who have gone through similar experiences and have found effective ways to combat feelings of isolation. In this Chapter I'll be exploring some strategies that can help you flourish and connect successfully with others in the solo parenting community.

First and foremost, it's crucial to reach out for support. Connect with other solo parents through local support groups, online forums, or social media communities. These networks can provide a safe space for sharing experiences, seeking advice, and finding solidarity with others who understand your unique challenges. By connecting with people who have walked a similar path, you can gain invaluable emotional support and practical insights.

Additionally, consider seeking professional help if you find yourself struggling with feelings of isolation. A therapist or counsellor can provide a non-judgmental space for you to express your emotions, process your thoughts, and develop coping strategies. They can also guide you in identifying and addressing any underlying issues that may be contributing to your sense of isolation.

Finding activities and hobbies that bring you joy and fulfillment is another great way to combat feelings of isolation. Engaging in activities that you enjoy not only helps you develop a sense of purpose but also provides opportunities to meet new people who share similar interests. Join local clubs, take up a new sport, or attend workshops and classes to expand your social circle and find companionship.

Lastly, it's important to prioritise self-care. As a solo parent, it's easy to neglect your own well-being while focusing on the needs of your children. However, taking care of yourself is pivotal in combating feelings of isolation. Make time for activities that recharge and rejuvenate you, such as practicing mindfulness, exercising, or indulging in a hobby you love. By prioritising self-care, you will not only feel more connected to yourself but also increase your capacity to connect with others.

You're not alone in this journey. By reaching out for support, seeking professional help, engaging in activities you enjoy, and prioritising self-care, you can combat feelings of isolation and build a strong support network of like-minded individuals who will help and support you.

ENGAGING IN COMMUNITY ACTIVITIES AND ORGANISATIONS

After going through a divorce, the journey of solo parenting can feel overwhelming and isolating. However, one of the most effective ways to navigate this new chapter of your life is by actively engaging in community activities and organisations. Not only can this help you build a strong support network, but it can also provide you with a sense of belonging and purpose.

When it comes to single parenting finding like-minded individuals who understand your struggles and challenges can make a world of difference. By joining community activities and organisations specifically catered to solo parents, you can connect with people who have gone through similar experiences and gain valuable insights and advice.

One of the first steps is to research local support groups or organisations that focus on providing resources and assistance to solo parents. These groups often offer counselling services, parenting classes, and even social events where you can meet other single parents in your area. Additionally, some organisations may provide financial aid or scholarships for single parents pursuing higher education or career opportunities.

Engaging in community activities not only benefits you but also your children. By participating in local events or programs, you expose your children to diverse experiences and opportunities for personal growth. They can develop social skills, build friendships, and learn from positive role models within the community. Moreover, involving your children in community service projects can teach them the importance of giving back and instill a sense of empathy and compassion.

Beyond support groups and community organisations, consider joining recreational clubs or sports teams that align with your interests and hobbies. This not only allows you to pursue your passions but also offers opportunities to meet new people and expand your social circle. Whether it's joining a book club, taking up a painting class, or becoming part of a running group, these activities can provide a much-needed break from the daily challenges of solo parenting.

Engaging in community activities and organisations is an essential part of thriving as a solo parent after divorce. It offers a platform to share experiences, seek guidance, and build a support system that can be invaluable on this journey. Remember, you don't have to face the challenges alone – there are communities waiting to welcome you with open arms. Embrace the opportunities that come with engaging in your community, and watch yourself and your children flourish as you navigate this new chapter of your life.

One of the most challenging aspects is feeling like you're alone in your struggles. It can be overwhelming to navigate this new chapter of your life without the support and understanding of others who have been through a similar experience. That's where solo parenting groups come in – they provide a safe and welcoming space for solo parents to connect, share their stories, and offer each other support.

SEEKING SUPPORT FROM SOLO PARENTING GROUPS

Solo parenting groups are specifically designed to cater to the unique needs of individuals who find themselves raising children on their own after a divorce. These groups understand the emotional, financial, and logistical challenges that solo parents face, and they aim to provide a sense of community and understanding.

Joining a solo parenting group can have numerous benefits. Firstly, it allows you to connect with others who are going through the same journey. You can share your experiences, exchange advice, and learn from each other's successes and failures. This sense of camaraderie can provide immense comfort, knowing that you're not alone in your struggles.

Secondly, solo parenting groups often invite guest speakers or professionals who can provide valuable insights and guidance on various aspects of solo parenting. From legal matters to co-parenting strategies, these sessions can equip you with the knowledge and tools you need to thrive as a solo parent.

Additionally, solo parenting groups can serve as a platform for building new friendships. It's not uncommon for lifelong friendships to form within these groups, as the shared experiences create a strong bond. Having friends who understand the challenges you face and can offer support and encouragement can make a world of difference in your solo parenting journey.

To find a solo parenting group in your area, start by reaching out to local community centres, or online forums dedicated to single parenting after divorce. It's important to find a group that aligns with your specific needs and values, so don't be afraid to try out a few different ones before settling on the right fit.

Seeking support from solo parenting groups is a courageous step towards ensuring your own well-being and that of your children.

By connecting with others who *truly* understand your journey, you can find the strength and resilience to thrive as a solo parent and create a fulfilling life for yourself and your children.

Chapter 13

RECLAIMING YOUR LIFE AND PURSUING PERSONAL GOALS

REDISCOVERING YOUR PASSIONS AND HOBBIES

After going through a divorce and becoming a solo parent, it's easy to lose sight of who you are and what brings you joy. The responsibilities and challenges that come with solo parenting can consume your life, leaving little time for self-discovery and personal growth. However, it's crucial to remember that you're more than just a parent – you're an individual with passions and hobbies that deserve to be nurtured.

Rediscovering your passions and hobbies is an essential part of the healing process. It allows you to reconnect with yourself, find new sources of happiness, and regain a sense of purpose outside of your role as a parent. Here are five steps to help you rediscover your passions.

1. **Reflect on your past interests:** Take some time to think back to your pre-divorce life. What activities or hobbies brought you joy? Did you have any passions that you put aside during your marriage? Revisiting these interests can be a great starting point for rediscovery.

2. **Try new things:** Consider exploring new hobbies or activities that you've always been curious about. Step out of your comfort zone and take a cooking class, join a book club, or try your hand at painting. Exploring new interests can open up a whole new world of possibilities and help you discover hidden talents.

3. **Make time for yourself:** As a solo parent, it's easy to get caught up in the never-ending to-do list. However, it's crucial to take time out and carve out some time for your passions. Set aside dedicated time each week to indulge in activities that make you happy, whether it's reading a book, going for a run, or practicing yoga.

4. **Connect with like-minded individuals**: Seek out communities or groups that share your interests. Joining clubs or organisations related to your hobbies can provide a sense of camaraderie and support. Surrounding yourself with like-minded individuals who understand your journey can be immensely empowering.

5. **Embrace the journey:** Rediscovering your passions and hobbies is a process that takes time. Be patient with yourself and enjoy the journey of self-discovery. Embrace the opportunity to reconnect with your authentic self and embrace the joy that comes from pursuing your passions.

By nurturing your own interests and hobbies, you become a happier and more fulfilled individual, which in turn positively impacts your role as a solo parent. By taking the time to rediscover your passions, you're not only creating a better life for yourself but also setting an inspiring example for your children.

By making yourself a priority and embracing *your* passions, you can find renewed joy and purpose in your life.

BUILDING A SUPPORTIVE SOCIAL NETWORK

After going through a divorce, solo parenting can feel overwhelming and isolating. As a single parent, it's fundamental to build a strong and supportive social network to help you navigate this new chapter in your life. Let me now outline the importance of building such a network and provide practical tips on how to do so.

One of the most significant challenges parenting on your own is the feeling of being alone in your struggles. However, by creating a supportive social network, you can find comfort, guidance, and assistance when needed. Your network can consist of friends, family members, fellow solo parents, support groups, and even professionals such as therapists or counsellors.

To start building your social network, reach out to trusted friends and family members who can offer emotional support and understanding. Share your experiences and concerns with them, as they may have valuable advice or be willing to lend a helping hand. Additionally, consider joining support groups or online communities specifically designed for solo parents. These groups provide a safe space to vent, share experiences, and connect with others who understand the unique challenges you face.

Networking with fellow solo parents can be particularly beneficial. Seek out local solo parenting support groups or parenting classes in your area. These groups often organise social events or workshops, giving you an opportunity to meet other solo parents and build lasting friendships. By surrounding yourself with individuals who have similar experiences, you can gain valuable insights, learn coping strategies, and feel a sense of belonging.

Furthermore, do not hesitate to seek professional help if needed. Therapists or counsellors specialising in divorce or solo parenting can provide you with guidance, coping mechanisms, and emotional support. They can help you navigate the complexities of solo parenting and assist in developing strategies to overcome challenges.

Remember, building a supportive social network takes time and effort. Be patient with yourself and others as you establish these connections. Nurture your relationships, offer support when you can, and be open to receiving help when needed.

Building a supportive social network is essential for solo parents. It provides a sense of belonging, emotional support, and practical assistance. By reaching out to friends, family, fellow solo parents, and professionals, you can create a network that helps you thrive as a solo parent. Remember, you're not alone, and there are people out there who understand and are willing to support you on this journey.

SETTING AND ACHIEVING PERSONAL MILESTONES

Setting and achieving personal milestones to create a fulfilling and successful life for both yourself and your children is a really positive step. These milestones will not only help you regain control over your life but also serve as a foundation for your personal growth and happiness.

Setting personal milestones begins with self-reflection and identifying what truly matters to you. Consider the areas of your life that require improvement, such as your emotional well-being, career, relationships, and self-care. By understanding your desires and aspirations, you can set realistic and attainable goals that align with your values and priorities.

The first step towards achieving personal milestones is to break them down into smaller, actionable steps. This allows you to create a clear path forward and avoid feeling overwhelmed. For instance, if your goal is to improve your emotional well-being, you could start by incorporating daily mindfulness or meditation practices into your routine. Over time, you can gradually increase the duration or explore other therapeutic activities that resonate with you.

Personal milestones are unique to each individual. Avoid comparing your progress to others, as this can lead to feelings of inadequacy or self-doubt. Instead, focus on your own journey and celebrate even the smallest achievements. By acknowledging your accomplishments, you will stay motivated and inspired to continue moving forward.

Accountability plays an important role in achieving personal milestones. Consider finding a support system or joining a community of solo parents who understand your challenges and can offer guidance and encouragement. Sharing your goals with trusted friends or family members can also help keep you accountable and provide additional motivation.

Lastly, be flexible and open to adjusting your milestones as needed. Life is unpredictable, and circumstances may change along the way. Give yourself permission to reassess your goals and make necessary modifications to ensure they remain relevant and realistic.

In summary, setting and achieving personal milestones is crucial for navigating life after separation and divorce. By identifying what matters most to you, breaking down goals into actionable steps, avoiding comparison, seeking support, and remaining flexible, you can create a fulfilling and successful life for yourself and your children.

Keep in mind, every milestone achieved is a step closer to a brighter future.

Chapter 14

NAVIGATING DATING AND ROMANTIC RELATIONSHIPS

EXPLORING NEW RELATIONSHIPS

In the previous chapter we explored single life, now let's look at how to navigate *new* relationships. One of the most challenging aspects of single parenting is navigating the world of new relationships. As a solo parent, it's natural to feel hesitant and uncertain about opening up to the possibility of finding love again. However, exploring new relationships can be a valuable and enriching experience, both for yourself and for your children.

Before embarking on this journey, it's crucial to take the time to heal and rediscover yourself. Divorce can leave emotional scars, and it's essential to address any lingering pain or unresolved issues before entering into a new relationship. Engaging in self-care activities, therapy, and leaning on a support network can help in this healing process.

Once you feel ready, it's important to approach new relationships with caution and intention. Remember that your children are also adjusting to the changes brought about by divorce, and their emotional well-being should be a priority.

Introducing a new partner too soon may create confusion and instability for your children. Take the time to build a solid foundation with your new partner before involving your children in the relationship.

> Communication is key when blending families. Clear and open conversations with your new partner about your expectations, parenting styles, and the potential role they will play in your children's lives are essential. It's imperative that your new partner understands and respects the boundaries you have established for your children's well-being.

Additionally, maintaining a healthy co-parenting relationship with your ex-spouse could be helpful when exploring new relationships. This requires effective communication, mutual respect, and a commitment to prioritise the children's needs above personal conflicts. A harmonious co-parenting dynamic will provide stability and security for your children as they adjust to the changes in their family structure.

Lastly, trust your instincts. As a solo parent, you have developed a keen sense of judgment and intuition. If something feels off or if red flags arise, listen to your gut feelings and take the necessary steps to protect yourself and your children.

Exploring new relationships can be both exciting and overwhelming. By taking the time to heal, communicate effectively, and prioritise your children's needs, you can create a fulfilling and balanced life for yourself and your family.

Remember, you deserve love and companionship just as much as anyone else, and your children can benefit from seeing you happy and thriving.

INTRODUCING A NEW PARTNER TO YOUR CHILDREN

One of the most challenging aspects is navigating the introduction of a new partner to your children. As a solo parent, you want to ensure that your children feel loved, secure, and comfortable in their changing family dynamics. Let's explore some valuable insights and practical tips on how to introduce a new partner to your children in a way that minimises stress and maximises their emotional well-being.

It's really important to remember that timing is critical Rushing into introducing a new partner too soon can overwhelm your children and potentially strain your relationship with them. Take the time to establish a solid foundation with your new partner before involving your children. This will allow you to build trust and ensure that the relationship is stable enough to withstand the challenges of blending families.

When the time feels right, have an open and honest conversation with your children about your new partner. Be sensitive to their emotions and reassure them that your love for them remains unchanged. Encourage them to express their feelings and concerns, and validate their emotions. It's very important for children to feel heard and understood during this transition.

Next, plan an initial meeting between your children and your new partner in a neutral and relaxed setting. This could be a casual outing or a fun activity that allows everyone to bond and get to know each other. Keep the first meeting brief, and avoid putting pressure on anyone to form an instant connection. Remember, relationships take time to develop, and it's essential to respect everyone's pace.

As the relationship progresses, gradually increase the amount of time your children spend with your new partner. Encourage open communication and ensure that your children feel comfortable expressing any concerns or reservations they may have. It's really important to address these concerns and provide reassurance, emphasising that their feelings are valid and respected.

Finally, aim for consistency and routine in your new family dynamics. Establish clear boundaries, rules, and expectations for everyone involved. This will provide a sense of stability and security for your children as they adjust to the changes in their lives.

Introducing a new partner to your children is a *significant* milestone in your solo parenting journey. By approaching it with patience, sensitivity, and open communication, you can create a harmonious blended family that thrives in the face of change.

BALANCING LOVE AND PARENTING RESPONSIBILITIES

When you find yourself navigating the world of solo parenting after a divorce, it can be overwhelming to juggle both your responsibilities as a parent and your desire for love and companionship. It's natural to feel torn between focusing on your children and seeking a fulfilling relationship for yourself. However, it's possible to strike a balance between these two important aspects of your life. Here are some strategies for you to look at.

You must prioritise your children's well-being. As a solo parent, your children depend on you for stability and support. Ensure you have established a solid foundation for them before pursuing a new romantic relationship. This may involve setting clear boundaries and routines, providing emotional support, and maintaining open communication with your children. By doing so, you can create a stable and secure environment that will allow you to pursue a new relationship without neglecting your parenting duties.

Additionally, it's important to be selective when it comes to introducing a new partner to your children. Take your time getting to know someone before involving them in your children's lives. Consider their values, compatibility with your family dynamics, and commitment to supporting your children's well-being. It may be wise to wait until you have established a strong foundation with your new partner before introducing them to your children. This approach will help ensure that your children's emotional needs are met, and they have a chance to adjust gradually to the changes in their family structure.

Furthermore, effective communication is important in balancing love and parenting responsibilities. Be open and honest with your new partner about your role as a parent and the time commitments it entails. Discuss your expectations and ensure that they understand and respect your responsibilities. By having these conversations early on, you can avoid misunderstandings and potential conflicts down the road.

Remember, you're not alone in this journey. Seek support from other solo parents who have successfully balanced love and parenting. Join support groups or online communities where you can exchange experiences, gain insights, and find encouragement. Connecting with others who have faced similar challenges can provide you with valuable advice and a sense of camaraderie.

Balancing love and parenting responsibilities requires careful consideration and planning. By prioritising your children's well-being, being selective in introducing new partners, practicing effective communication, and seeking support from others, you can successfully navigate this delicate balancing act.

Don't forget, it's *absolutely* possible to find love and happiness while being a dedicated and loving parent.

Chapter 15

CELEBRATING YOUR STRENGTHS AND ACCOMPLISHMENTS

REFLECTING ON YOUR JOURNEY

As a single parent it's essential to take the time to reflect on your journey. Reflecting allows you to gain insight, learn from your experiences, and grow as an individual. Let me share the importance of self-reflection and provide you with practical tips to help you reflect on your unique journey.

Reflection is a powerful tool that helps you make sense of the past and create a brighter future. It allows you to identify patterns, strengths, and areas for improvement.

> By reflecting on your journey, you can gain a deeper understanding of yourself as a parent and the impact of divorce on your life. It's an opportunity to celebrate your resilience, acknowledge your challenges, and appreciate your growth.

To begin your reflection, find a quiet and comfortable space where you can be alone with your thoughts. Start by acknowledging your emotions and allowing yourself to feel them fully. Recognise the progress you have made since the divorce and the strength it takes to raise your child(ren) on your own.

Next, consider your parenting journey. Look back on the moments when you felt proud, competent, and connected with your children. What strategies or approaches worked well for you during those times? Write them down and remind yourself of these strengths as you face future challenges.

Equally important, reflect on the moments when you faced difficulties or made mistakes. Be gentle with yourself and recognise that everyone makes mistakes. Use these moments as opportunities for growth and learning. Consider what you could have done differently and how you can apply those lessons moving forward.

It's also beneficial to think about your personal growth outside of parenting. Have you developed any new skills or hobbies? How have you prioritised self-care and your own well-being? Reflecting on these aspects of your journey will help you see the progress you have made in rebuilding your life as a solo parent.

Finally, remember that reflection is an ongoing process. Set aside regular time for self-reflection to ensure you continue to learn and grow. Consider keeping a journal or finding a support group where you can share your reflections with others who understand your journey.

Reflecting on your journey is a powerful tool for personal growth and empowerment. Embrace the opportunity to learn from your experiences, celebrate your achievements, and navigate the challenges ahead with confidence.

ACKNOWLEDGING YOUR GROWTH AS A SOLO PARENT

As a solo parent navigating the challenging terrain of single parenthood after a divorce, it's crucial to take a moment to acknowledge and appreciate your personal growth. Let's remind ourselves on the journey you have embarked upon, the obstacles you have overcome, and the strength you have gained along the way.

Becoming a solo parent is undoubtedly one of life's greatest challenges. However, it's important to recognise that with every challenge comes an opportunity for growth. In the aftermath of a divorce, you may have experienced a range of emotions, from grief and loss to anger and confusion. But through it all, you have persevered, showing incredible resilience and strength.

One key aspect of acknowledging your growth as a solo parent is recognising the progress you have made in your parenting skills. Initially, you may have doubted your ability to handle your children's needs on your own. However, as time goes on, you will see how far you have come. From managing schedules to comforting your children during tough times, you have developed a newfound confidence in your parenting abilities.

Another area of growth to acknowledge is the personal development you have undergone. As a solo parent, you have taken on new responsibilities and faced challenges head-on. You have learned to juggle multiple roles, from being the primary caregiver to managing household finances. Through this process, you have become more self-reliant, resourceful, and independent.

Furthermore, your emotional growth as a solo parent should not be overlooked. Divorce can be emotionally draining, leaving you feeling vulnerable and uncertain about the future. However, as you navigate the ups and downs of single parenthood, you have learned to become more emotionally resilient. You have developed coping mechanisms, sought support from friends and family, and discovered inner strength you may not have known existed.

Finally, acknowledging your growth as a solo parent means celebrating the milestones you have achieved. Whether it's successfully co-parenting with your ex-spouse, finding a better work-life balance, or simply making it through a particularly challenging week, each small victory deserves recognition. By acknowledging your growth, you can boost your self-esteem and gain the confidence needed to thrive as a solo parent.

The journey of solo parenting is undoubtedly a daunting one. However, by taking the time to acknowledge and appreciate your growth, you can embrace your new role with confidence and strength. Remember that you're not alone on this journey, and the challenges you face only serve to make you a stronger, more resilient individual.

EMBRACING A POSITIVE FUTURE

Parenting alone can be overwhelming. It's natural to feel a mix of emotions, including fear, sadness, and uncertainty about the future. However, it's important to remember that you have the power to shape a positive future for yourself and your children. Let's look at some strategies and mindset shifts that can help you embrace a positive future.

1. **Cultivate a Positive Mindset:** Your mindset plays an important role in shaping your future. Instead of dwelling on negative thoughts or the past, focus on the opportunities that lie ahead. Train yourself to see challenges as opportunities for growth and view setbacks as stepping stones towards a better future. Surround yourself with positive influences, practice gratitude, and celebrate small victories along the way.

2. **Set Realistic Goals:** Take time to define your goals and aspirations for yourself and your children. Break them down into smaller, achievable steps, and create a roadmap to guide you. Remember to set realistic expectations and be flexible in adapting your plans as needed. By having a clear vision for the future, you can stay motivated and focused on creating a positive life for yourself and your children.

3. **Prioritise Self-Care:** As a solo parent, it's easy to neglect self-care in the midst of busy schedules and parenting responsibilities. However, taking care of yourself is really important for your well-being and

your ability to provide for your children. Make time for activities that bring you joy, practice self-compassion, and seek support from friends, family, or support groups.

4. **Foster Strong Relationships:** Building a support network can be really beneficial. Surround yourself with individuals who uplift and understand your journey. Seek out other solo parents through local support groups or online communities. Share experiences, advice, and resources to help each other thrive. Additionally, foster positive relationships with your co-parent, if possible, by focusing on effective communication and co-parenting strategies that prioritise the well-being of your children.

5. **Embrace New Beginnings**: Divorce marks the end of one chapter but also opens the door to new beginnings. Embrace the opportunity to create a new life for yourself and your children. Explore new hobbies, pursue personal and professional growth, and create new traditions. Your ability to adapt and embrace change will not only empower you but also inspire your children to approach life's challenges with resilience and optimism.

Embracing a positive future requires effort and self-belief. By cultivating a positive mindset, setting realistic goals, prioritising self-care, fostering strong relationships, and embracing new beginnings, you can create a fulfilling and thriving life for yourself and your children.

Don't forget, there is a community of solo parents who are navigating this journey alongside you so take advantage and seek support.

CONCLUSION

Congratulations! You've now reached the end of *Thriving Alone: A Guide to Solo Parenting After Divorce,* and have taken the first step towards embracing your solo parenting journey. As a solo parent, you have embarked on a unique path that comes with its own set of challenges and triumphs. Remember, you're not alone in this journey, and countless others have walked this path before you.

Throughout this book, we've explored various aspects of solo parenting, providing you with valuable insights, practical tips, and emotional support. We have touched upon the initial stages of adjusting to your new role, managing co-parenting relationships, nurturing your child's emotional well-being, and taking care of your own self-care needs.

The journey of a single parent isn't an easy one, but it's filled with immense growth and self-discovery. It's a time when you can truly focus on yourself and your child, creating a nurturing and loving environment. You have the power to shape your child's future and provide them with the love and support they need.

It's critical to understand that you cannot do it all alone. Seek support from friends, family, or support groups specifically tailored for solo parents. Surround yourself with a network of people who understand your unique challenges and can offer guidance and encouragement when needed. Seeking help isn't a sign of weakness but a sign of strength.

Take time to recharge and rejuvenate yourself so that you can be the best parent possible. Find activities that bring you joy and help alleviate stress. Whether it's exercising, journaling, or pursuing a hobby, make sure you have time set aside for yourself.

Lastly, embrace the journey of solo parenting. It may not be the path you initially envisioned, but it's a chance to grow and thrive independently. Celebrate your accomplishments, big or small, and give yourself credit for the incredible job you're doing.

The journey may be challenging, but it's also an opportunity for personal growth, self-discovery, and creating a beautiful life for yourself and your child. As I've reminded you throughout this book, you're not alone in this journey, and there is a community of solo parents ready to offer support and encouragement. Embrace this new chapter of your life, and may your solo parenting journey be filled with love, joy, and endless possibilities.

WHERE NEXT?

If you have found the information in this book useful, then why don't you come and join my facebook community, Thriving Alone: Support after Separation and Divorce.

Or simply scan the QR below.

ABOUT THE AUTHOR

Lynn is an ex military wife and a mum of three who found herself going through a divorce after 22 years of marriage.

She suddenly found herself solo parenting, without her ex husband and without the army community. This also included leaving the army home where they lived as a family with their three children.

This was her first step to navigating life as a single mum.

Lynn now runs a successful business and helps other women to navigate life after separation. *Thriving Alone: A guide to solo parenting after divorce* is her first book, and she wrote it to help guide parents through this difficult and often emotionally charged time.

She lives in Northumberland with her three children and their dog, Ollie.

Printed in Great Britain
by Amazon